Saving the World
One Word at a Time:
Writing Cli-Fi

Also by
Ellen Briana Szabo

Love and Apocalypse:
Externalize Your Inner Apocalypse with Creative Writing

Saving the World
One Word at a Time
Writing Cli-Fi

Ellen Briana Szabo

http://www.justwritenow.org/
@ebszabo
words@justwritenow.org

Edited by Barbara Siergiewicz, Victoria Bennet,
Martha Schut, Doug Peters
Design by Laura Friedland
Photography by Ellen Briana Szabo

First Edition 2015

YELLOW ISLAND PRESS

Yellow Island Press
Gloucester

For my children who taught me love and humility,
and for an old friend.

Acknowledgements

If we want to be happy, what choice do we have when something happens, but to find gratitude for the bad as well as the good? This book was written because I wanted to be happy – so heartfelt thanks to the constellation of people and events that led me to write the apocalypse, and to emerge from living it, to putting it behind me, for good.

Table of Contents

Preface

I wrote Love and Apocalypse and Saving the World One Word at a Time in response to requests from clients and students for writing prompts that inspired personal transformation and social advocacy.

I have been teaching *Creative Writing for Social Work* at the University of Iowa, School of Social Work since 1999. Thanks to the faculty and administration who have supported this workshop, to guest speakers who enhanced and provided depth to the range of topics covered, and to class participants who brought creativity and enthusiasm each year, I have been able to develop and enhance a curriculum that explores the uses of creative writing for personal investigation and social activism.

It wasn't until I began researching and writing about an apocalyptic world, that I fully appreciated the power of creative writing to externalize my inner apocalypse. This process led me to a deep appreciation for the literary genre of speculative fiction (more about that later), and an unexpected fascination with science and physics. I wish someone had told me when I was young that separation of the 'hard sciences' and 'creative arts' was a false duality, a revelation that has changed how I perceive and write about myself and the world.

Writing fiction can be a nonthreatening way to process information that we might otherwise shut out to protect ourselves, it can help us to imagine something better, and it offers ways to make sense of the world. It can inspire and transform.

This book celebrates the intersection of creative writing, personal transformation, social activism and healing, and is an invitation to write at that intersection.

Ellen Briana Szabo, June 2015

Writing for Change

I've always been an avid reader – when I was in elementary and middle school, my parents worried that I was spending too much time with books and too little time making friends. I was introverted, (and in retrospect, depressed). Reading provided escape, and a sense of belonging.

Then, in high school, I discovered social activism.

My parents raised me to have a social conscience. My father gladly wrote me notes for excused absences when I was in high school so that I could participate in peace demonstrations in Harvard Square in the late 1960s, early 70s. I confess I didn't spend all of my absences in protest marches, but I came pretty close. I worked for ecology action groups to raise consciousness about saving the planet. I canvassed for Eugene McCarthy for president and collected signatures for '18 by 72', the movement to lower the voting age to eighteen by 1972. That movement succeeded, and when I turned eighteen I was able to vote in the presidential election.

My father's ancestors, like Dracula, came from Transylvania, and perhaps that explains why I've always loved dark, dystopian and apocalyptic literature. In middle school I discovered Mary Shelley's Frankenstein (1818) then Charlotte Bronte's Jane Eyre (1847), Emily Bronte's Wuthering Heights (1847), and Braham Stoker's Dracula (1897), to name a few. All of these writers incorporated elements of social criticism (and bad weather) into complex stories about monsters and monstrous people. I went on to discover more contemporary writers, one of my favorites being Margaret Atwood, all of whom wrote provocative stories with elegance and depth. I did love a good love story, but only if it was embedded in disaster.

Still, I didn't understand the degree to which fiction could be an agent of social change.

As I researched the significance of weather as a theme in fiction, I discovered that Mary Shelley wrote Frankenstein during a year of weather so extreme that some referred to it as "The Year Without Summer".[1] A volcanic eruption in Indonesia filled the atmosphere with dust, triggering severe weather in Europe and North America. Skies were dark for weeks, it was dangerously cold, harvests failed, resulting in food riots and starvation deaths.

Shelley's references to frightful storms evoked weather as darkly threatening as Frankenstein's legendary monster. Equally striking was the far-reaching impact of that natural disaster. The ecological, economic, and social fallout of a volcanic eruption demonstrates the potentially global influence of seemingly localized triggers for weather events and conditions.

In recent decades, the facts and consequences of climate change have become increasingly difficult to ignore. The question of whether or not climate change is anthropocentric (caused by humans) is hotly contested in the public arena. It appears that for many people, beliefs about climate change and global warming are influenced by political orientation and ideology, rather than science. A significant number of Americans say they do not believe that climate change is anthropocentric, and many report that they don't believe climate change is actually occurring.

---

[1] August 13, 2007, *NPR, Special Series: Signs,* "Did Climate Inspire the Birth of a Monster?" Nell Greenfieldboyce, http://www.npr.org/templates/story/story.php?storyId=12688403 .

Media reporting on climate change has emphasized disastrous trends and catastrophic events, probably because this makes stories interesting and captures attention. But all that bad news can manifest a pervasive and paralyzing sense of helplessness. If we feel helpless to make meaningful change, we are likely to feel hopeless and to give up. It's not enough to be informed. We must have a sense of agency, a belief in our capacity to exert influence. Activism by its very nature implies a deeply held belief that things can be better – and that we can do something to make that happen.

Otherwise, why bother?

I never realized that writing fiction could be useful in that sense.

Fiction can be a nonthreatening way to identify threats and injustice. It is a venue detached from the real world, where disaster and suspense are exciting because they are vicarious. This allows us to process information that we might otherwise shut out to protect ourselves. Fiction can also help us to imagine something better, by offering insight, and suggesting ways to make sense of the world. Writing and reading are personal, even intimate, acts, and perhaps because of this, fiction can access consciousness and conscience more effectively than a stern lecture or dire predictions based on fact. Good fiction and inspiring characters can prompt personal transformation and even social change.

It turns out, writing Speculative fiction can be a form of social activism. Speculative fiction is characterized by inventive, imaginary expressions of speculated outcomes for social, ecological and scientific developments. A growing number of scientists and writers are turning to this genre as a medium for important messages about climate change. Cli-fi (abbreviation for climate fiction), has recently been articulated and advocated as a distinct literary genre by freelance writer Dan Bloom.[2]

Cli-Fi is speculative fiction that focuses primarily on the ways that climate change is transforming our world. It is a literary genre with a mission – to transform our future from worst case predictions to best case scenarios, by changing how we humans think about, inhabit and interact with our planet. By anticipating and elaborating on the implications of climate change in the not so distant future, many writers of cli-fi use knowledge of science and climate to imagine and create apocalyptic or dystopian worlds that we hope will remain fiction. The best cli-fi seamlessly intertwines literary fabrication and science; it's a literary collaboration between the disciplines of science and the humanities.

Cli-fi offers opportunities to reimagine the message and the messengers of climate change, taking the issue into the realm of the personal (and vicarious). An underlying message of hope – no matter how subtle – can give a sense of purpose and agency to a fictional apocalypse. This is why character development in cli-fi is of utmost importance. And why having a mission statement for your story is essential.

If the reader can identify with someone, and believe there is reason to stay with them, then they are likely to consider a scary story worth reading. Think of your characters as the foot soldiers of your mission.

---

[2] Cli-fi Guy http://northwardho.blogspot.com/2015/02/cli-fi-guy.html and The Cli-fi Report, http://cli-fi.net/index.html.

This book can get you started with writing prompts, resources, and recommended readings intended to guide, provoke, and inspire you as you tackle saving the world one word at a time.

When you write cli-fi consider these points:

- Base your story on an *outcome scenario* that could conceivably happen as a result of one or more aspects of climate change if remedies aren't put in place.
- *Research* is essential, and resources abound (see Recommended Resources)
- When you *create an altered world,* make it as extreme as you wish, but *embed the familiar* to make it feel true.
- Populate the world with *characters* your reader will want to spend time with.
- Giving your story a mission can offer your reader a sense of purpose and agency.

Apokálypsis

As you formulate the mission for your story, consider this: the word *apocalypse*, translated from the Greek *apokálypsis,* means revelation of knowledge.

Your story's mission helps you to articulate the change you want to inspire in your readers. It can help to guide the decisions you make about characters and events. It can help you to separate what's important and what's not.

You may not be able to identify the mission statement of your cli-fi story right away, but usually it will derive from a personal experience that has shaped the 'why' of what you do, giving your struggle purpose.

A mission statement might read something like this: *This story about the extinction of the passenger pigeon will awaken*

people to the dangers of unbridled technology and the need for compassion and foresight in implementing all technological advances.

Free Writing

Free-writes will be valuable to you as you write your cli-fi story and populate it with characters that must wrestle with demons in their internal and external world.

When you feel stuck in the story, or if you are struggling with who a character is, free writing can help you to discover vibrant, meaningful material.

Some suggestions for getting the most out of your writing:

- For each writing prompt, commit to writing for *at least* ten minutes.
- Don't stop to think, don't re-read. Just write.
- Don't worry about spelling, punctuation, grammar, or sentence structure.
- Don't be polite, write what you see and feel, not what you think you should see and feel.
- If you do better with lists, write in list form, if you do better with email write in an email, get as freed up as you can – your best material comes from creative freedom, not from obeying rules.
- Break the rules about writing that you learned in school.

From here we will venture into developing ideas for plot, place and character in cli-fi.

Climate Change

Prompt: In a 10 minute free-write, list everything the words *climate change* evoke for you.

Pivot

Prompt: Write for at least ten minutes about a pivotal event in your life that changed how you perceive yourself and your world. What led up to this event? What was its significance to you? Do you think about it differently now than you did at the time? Were other people involved? In what way did they shape your experience of the event?

Terms

Prompt: Now consider that event and write for at least ten minutes about the consequences and how you have (or have not) come to terms with them.

Lies

Prompt: Write a list of "Lies that changed the world."

Plot

Plot is more than just what happens.

Plot is built from significant events in a story that have important consequences.

In a strong, textured story, there are plots and subplots.

In cli-fi the main plot will be based on long term consequences of climate change. It might be how city life is threatened when climate change has interrupted the migration patterns of animals and birds, or how rising sea levels have altered the coastline and lifestyle of a small fishing town.

When considering plot, give yourself time to research what interests you – for example, when I was working on a story set in Manhattan, I discovered that the Manhattan of the 1600s was known for its wolves. This fascinated me. What happened to them? Where did they go if they survived? An American horror film about mutated wolves in 1980s Manhattan scared the daylights out of me. I was living in Manhattan at the time and thankfully didn't know that wolves had once been native to that area. Who's to say they aren't still hidden there? That discovery gave me a basis for the inclusion of wolves in the story I set in Manhattan of the future.

Prompt: Research the history of a city or town you are thinking of using for your story location. See what you can find out about the natural habitat decades or centuries ago. Incorporate what you discover into a free write, use your imagination and create a future scenario in which the natural habitat or inhabitants return with consequences.

Subplots

Subplots can help to personalize the story – they may involve relationships between parent and child, between siblings or friends, between lovers, or complete strangers. Some subplots serve to illuminate the social structure of the world you create – they might involve a dispute between two polarized factions in a city neighborhood, or the strife created between siblings when one is elevated to a power position in the newly formed caste system, and the other is relegated to poverty.

Either way, subplots are embedded into the main story to provide emotional and social texture and dynamic. They serve your book's mission as they unfold, creating complications and resistance for your characters, demonstrating the meaning and purpose of the struggle, and the implications of failure.

Most of us lead ordinary lives, boundaried by habit, by how we earn (or don't earn) a living, and by the extent of our resources. Disaster can be an equalizer – and it can trigger exaggerated power and control systems. As you conceive of your cli-fi story consider whether the consequences of climate change will configure a new caste system. What will be the basis of wealth and power? What becomes scarce that was formerly plentiful? Food? Water? Chocolate? Ice? Internet access? Gasoline?

17

Prompt: Make a list of resources that you took for granted as a child. Then make a list of resources you take for granted today. Compare these lists and imagine a new economy in which a particular (unlikely) resource has become the basis for a new barter system, and a new economy. How does this reshape the caste system?

18

Foot Soldiers

As you populate your fictional world, keep in mind that your characters will have significant responsibility for the success of your story long after you've written it.

Each of these writing prompts can help you to discover candidates for your story – even if you don't yet know what the story is about, you'll find that characters volunteer themselves as you write. So scour the photographs provided in this book for details, respond to the questions, write freely – minutia matters, let the details tell you who you are writing about.

Give characters substance, fortitude, frailties and complexity. They must enact the story, as they march headlong into disaster, (after disaster after disaster,) while being so compelling that they can coax your readers, against better judgement, into the belly of the beast (over and over again).

Create sympathetic characters – give the reader reason to care about them by showing them in private moments doing something tender for someone. Then plunge them into chaos and danger.

Prompt: It can be interesting to tell a story from the perspective of an archeologist who analyzes artifacts and other remains and then pieces together stories to explain cultures and extinctions. Write about this face on a wall from the perspective of an archeologist who is working to understand what changed life on this planet in the twenty first century.

Chipper and Eddie

It's a good idea to start in the middle of things.

Consider opening your story with an event that hints at what the main problem will be without giving it away. This can give the reader a chance to get to know the main characters and a little about the world they are living in – and trouble to come. Whether the story begins after an apocalyptic event or before, let the reader witness a moment that defines 'life now'.

Prompt: Who are Chipper and Eddie? What unexpected event necessitated abandoning these boats? What happened to the person in the third boat? Write the scene immediately following a significant event that reveals a truth about these three people and their seemingly ordinary world.

Keeping Clean

Warming temperatures, changes in precipitation, and sea level rise are impacting water supplies and quality, and as demand for water increases, the supply diminishes.

How will this influence social behaviors and norms? Will keeping clean become unethical – a symbol of waste?

Prompt: Create a world where clean water is so valuable that cleanliness has become suspect. Perhaps even a criminal offense?

What You Know

How do you make the incredible feel plausible? By evoking the ordinary.

The advice 'write what you know' doesn't mean you can only write about a zombie apocalypse if you've actually experienced one. It means 'bring what you know to what you write'.

What happens in a zombie apocalypse can be experienced from inside a laundromat, for example.

Most of us have washed clothes before. We are familiar with the floral smell of laundry soap, and the way the powder crusts around the damp pour spout. There's the slosh and spin of water, and the trembling of the machines.

If you've used public washers and dryers you know what it's like to have to wait for a dryer, and count and recount quarters. Perhaps you've had to listen to the thump of sneakers tumbling inside a dryer drum while worrying that someone else will get the next available dryer before you do.

Or perhaps the zombie apocalypse begins inside a diner. The menus are sticky, the water is cloudy and there's dried mustard on the salt and pepper shakers. The smell of burnt coffee and hash browns clings to the vinyl upholstery and then there's the zombie reanimating in the booth across from your main character.

Prompt: Write about a cataclysmic event from the vantage point of an ordinary place. Use familiar details to ground the story, and to help your reader relate to the experience as if it could happen to them.

Trigger

Stories begin when whatever has worked for the main character is upset by a triggering event. That trigger sets things in motion that require your character to adapt. Which, of course she will fail to do. Her struggle propels the story forward.

Prompt: Introduce us to a character at the moment of 'trigger'. What message was written on the yellow lined paper? What call will she (or he) make? Locate this character in time and place, help us to get to know her by taking cues from these items on her bedside table.

Perspective

Every character has their own, distinct belief system. This means that no two characters will see or experience an event in the same way. This is a good thing because it creates conflicts and misunderstandings, and sets up unpredictable chemistries between characters – all of which make stories interesting and suspenseful.

So move now to the person who wrote the message on the yellow lined paper that triggered the crisis.

Prompt:

Build this character's belief system, and imagine him (or her) sitting in this chair as he writes. What drove him to write the message? Who is he? How did the stretchers (the horizontals between the legs) break? Why is the padlock unlocked? What will he do after he writes the note? What is his relationship with the character he writes it to? What difference in believe systems has led to this moment? Be curious, ask everything you can about this photograph, and apply what you decipher to creating the character.

Pockets

What people carry in their pockets can tell us a great deal about who they are and what they do.

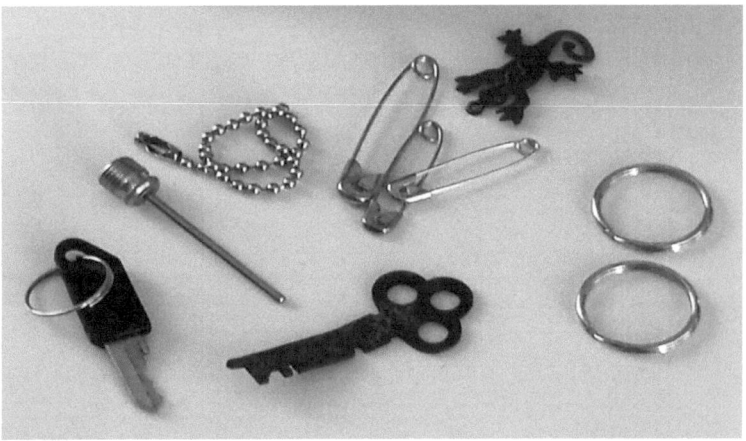

Prompt: Create the character who carries these items in her (or his) pockets. What does she do for a living? What does she do for fun that she was told never to do. What happens when she goes through a security checkpoint, and is flagged for questioning? Help us to learn about her through what she must hide during her exchange with security agents.

Begin Here

We are building a world we cannot live in.

Climate changes are impacting the distribution and behaviors of animals, birds and plants. We are seeing examples of this as animals such as mountain lions, coyotes, wolves and bears are being driven into cities and towns as they lose their natural habitats.

The migratory patterns of birds are also changing as a result of human behaviors – the passenger pigeon, once so plentiful their flights could darken the sky, became extinct one hundred years ago as a result of advancing human technologies. More recently, warming temperatures are causing changes in the migration patterns and breeding areas of Canada Geese. What are the implications of this?

Prompt: Write the opening paragraph for a story that begins at a construction site. Introduce the main character, show him (or her) working and bantering with his co-workers in the course of a regular day. Then incorporate a story of displaced birds, inspired by what you see in these two photographs.

Pollution, A Love Story

2014 was the hottest year on record. And everyone loves a love story.

Prompt: Select one observable effect of global climate change and imagine the long term consequences. Write the opening paragraph for <u>Pollution, A (Hot) Love Story.</u>

The World is Flat

Belief is more likely shaped by emotions than by facts. Perhaps this is why the facts of climate change are so hotly contested. And why emotional connection is imperative to change.

Prompt: Begin a story with this exchange:
"Well, that's just like telling me the world is flat."
"It sure looks flat from here."

Home Sweet Home

Anthropocentric climate change is causing increased extreme weather events around the globe, resulting in heat waves and coastal flooding.

Prompt: Who lives here? And Why? Create the story of a group of strangers who arrive here and must make it their home. Explore the ordinary moments when they must find ways to adapt – how will they prepare food? What will they use for bedding? How will they share the space equitably? Research various camping and first aid techniques and incorporate them into the story as people discover ways to coexist.

A Dark and Stormy

Don't lose your sense of humor.

Prompt: Begin a story with "It was a dark and stormy…" and include at least one science fact and at least one science fiction.

One Word at a Time

Prompt: Read through what you have generated from these writing prompts, you'll find fertile material with unlimited potential for cli-fi stories.

1. Select one or more of the free-writes and imagine them as a bigger story, do a new free-write on what the story is about.
2. Select a character to be your protagonist (main character), and then select an antagonist (the primary

opposition character). Get to know them by free-writing, using some of the prompts in this book.

3. Locate the story in a world of your creation, and animate it with characters who can fulfill your story's mission.
4. Research the science to support your fiction.
5. For additional guidance about creative writing, go to www.justwritenow.org

The better we write, the farther the reach and impact of our stories.

Creative Writing for Social Work

The annual *Creative Writing for Social Workers* seminar emphasizes improving creative writing skills while exploring the uses of creative writing for personal investigation and social change.

For information:

Creative Writing for Social Workers at the University of Iowa School of Social Work

Recommended Resources

Readings

Curry, Judith, "Christopher Essex on Suppressing Scientific Inquiry." *Climate Etc. Blog*, March 26, 2015 http://judithcurry.com/2015/03/26/christopher-essex-on-suppressing-scientific-inquiry/#more-18220.

Klein, Naomi, *This Changes Everything; Capitalism vs the Climate*, New York: Simon and Schuster, 2014.

Lamott, Anne. Bird by Bird: Some Instructions on Writing and Life. New York: Pantheon Books, 1994.

Monosson, Emily, *Evolution in a Toxic World; How Life Responds to Chemical Threats,* Washington, D.C.: Island Press, 2012.

Oreskes, Naomi and Conway, Erik M., *Merchants of Doubt; How A Handful of Scientists Obscured the Truth on Issues from Tobacco Smoke to Global Warming*, New York: Bloomsbury Press, 2010 *www.merchantsofdoubt.org* .

Greenfieldboyce, Nell, "Did Climate Inspire the Birth of a Monster?" *NPR, Special Series: Signs* August 13, 2007. http://www.npr.org/templates/story/story.php?storyId=12688403

Websites

Inside Climate News http://insideclimatenews.org/ winner of Pulitzer Prize for National Reporting.

"Science Fiction and Fantasy" *NPR Books*, http://www.npr.org/books/genres/10119/science-fiction-fantasy/?ps=books_nav_scifi.

Goodreads, https://www.goodreads.com/search?utf8=%E2%9C%93&query=climate+fiction.

Bloom, Daniel *Cli-Fi* http://northwardho.blogspot.com/2015/02/cli-fi-guy.html.

Yale Project on Climate Change Communication; Bridging Science and Society
  http://environment.yale.edu/climate-communication/ .

Speculative Fiction

Atwood, Margaret, *Oryx and Crake,* New York: Nan Talese/Doubleday, 2003.

Atwood, Margaret, *The Year of the Flood,* New York: Nan Talese/Doubleday, 2009.

Atwood, Margaret, *Maddaddam,* New York: Nan Talese/Doubleday, 2013.

Jensen, Liz, *The Rapture,* New York: Doubleday, 2009

McCarthy, Cormac, *The Road*, New York: Alfred Knopf/Random House, 2006.

Oreskes, Naomi and Conway, Erik M., *The Collapse of Western Civilization; A View from the Future*, New York: Columbia University Press, 2014.

Shelley, Mary, *Frankenstein*, New York: Dover, 1994, (republication of the text of third edition of 1831, London, Colburn and Bentley).

Walker, Karen Thompson, *The Age of Miracles,* New York: Random House, 2012.

Whitehead, Colson, *Zone 1*, New York: Doubleday/Random House, 2011.

Going Green

- Recycle glass, aluminum, plastic and paper, old cell phones
- Turn off computers at night instead of leaving on 'sleep mode'
- Get a clothesline and hang clothes to dry
- Wash in cold or warm instead of hot water
- Go vegetarian (in addition to sparing animals, this saves water and trees)
- Use both sides of paper
- Use cloth instead of paper napkins (some, if not all, of the time)
- Wrap creatively – reuse gift bags, ribbons, maps, magazines, newspaper and grocery bags
- Reduce water usage: shower instead of bathe
- Plant a tree – improves air quality and provides shade to save on cooling
- Brush teeth without running water, only to rinse.
- Buy second hand – at thrift or consignment shops
- Buy local
- Batch errands
- Adjust your thermostat
- If you have cruise control, use it
- Greener lawn care: water less, and do it early in the morning, spot treat weeds with vinegar, implement xeriscape gardening

About the Author

Ellen Briana Szabo practices and promotes the use of creative writing for personal investigation, enrichment and social change. She earned her B.A. from Harvard College, with a concentration in English and American Literature, and her M.Ed. from Columbia University Teacher's College, in Counseling Psychology. She writes and teaches with focus on how innovation and creativity can illuminate, inspire and advocate compassionate transformation. She teaches Creative Writing for Social Work at the University of Iowa, School of Social Work. Her private practice is based in Massachusetts, providing creative writing instruction, coaching, editing and support to individuals and groups, locally and online.

www.ingramcontent.com/pod-product-compliance
Lightning Source LLC
Chambersburg PA
CBHW050753290526
45792CB00008B/2163